THE UNSTOPPABLE YOU

MAXWELL MOMENTS

THE UNSTOPPABLE YOU

7 WAYS TO TAP INTO YOUR POTENTIAL FOR SUCCESS

JOHN C. MAXWELL

CENTER STREET

Nashville • New York

The author is represented by Yates & Yates, LLP, Literary Agency, Santa Ana, California.

Center Street
Hachette Book Group
1290 Avenue of the Americas, New York, NY 10104
centerstreet.com
twitter.com/centerstreet

First Edition: March 2023

Center Street is a division of Hachette Book Group, Inc. The Center Street name and logo are trademarks of Hachette Book Group, Inc.

The publisher is not responsible for websites (or their content) that are not owned by the publisher.

The Hachette Speakers Bureau provides a wide range of authors for speaking events. To find out more, go to www.HachetteSpeakersBureau.com or call (866) 376-6591.

Print book interior design by Bart Dawson.

Scripture quotations are taken from the *New Life Version*, copyright © 1969 and 2003. Used by permission of Barbour Publishing, Inc., Uhrichsville, Ohio 44683. All rights reserved.

Library of Congress Cataloging-in-Publication Data has been applied for.

ISBNs: 9781546002543 (paperback), 9781546002550 (ebook)

Printed in the United States of America

LSC-C

Printing 1, 2022

CONTENTS

DON'T LET ANYONE LIMIT YOU—ESPECIALLY YOU!

"KNOW THYSELF."

—Socrates

What's keeping you from doing the things you really want to do?

What's stopping you from attaining the success you desire?

What's preventing you from reaching your full potential and achieving your dreams?

Everyone has limitations put on them by others. Everyone faces challenges. Everyone possesses limitations of their own. But what if those aren't your greatest obstacles?

What if your greatest problem is you—and you don't even know it?

Most people believe they are more limited than they actually are.

They never bump their head against the ceiling of their limitations because they never reach high enough to hit it.

"We don't have a clue as to what people's limits are. All the tests, stopwatches, and finish lines in the world can't measure human potential. When someone is pursuing their dream, they'll go far beyond what seems to be their limitations. The potential that exists within us is limitless and largely untapped."

—Robert Kriegel and Louis Patler

Your potential is not fixed. Your limitations don't limit you nearly as much as you think they do. The main reason you're not unstoppable may be that you're stopping yourself. You need to become open to the possibilities that are within you.

Don't limit your own capacity.

"*I THINK SELF-KNOWLEDGE IS THE RAREST TRAIT IN A HUMAN BEING.*"

—Elizabeth Edwards

How do you move from self-limiting to unstoppable?

The first step is self-awareness.

Knowing yourself is powerful. It enables you to see yourself clearly. It informs your decisions and helps you weigh opportunities. It allows you to test your limits. It empowers you to understand other people. It makes partnerships with others stronger. It allows you to maximize your strengths and minimize your weaknesses.

It opens the door to greater capacity.

The second step is focusing on your strengths.

Maybe you already know this. When you focus on improving your weaknesses, the best you can do is work your way up to average. Nobody is unstoppable when working in weaknesses. Success comes from doing what you do with excellence. Excellence comes from working in your strengths. Whatever you do well, try to do better.

That's your greatest pathway forward to increased capacity.

The third step is to be willing to push your own boundaries.

That's what Henry Ford had to do—literally. In the mid-1890s, Ford began building his first vehicle with bicycle parts and a combustion engine. He worked on it in a shop behind the rental house where he and his wife lived. When he completed his project, he called his vehicle the quadricycle. However, he'd made one small miscalculation: It was too big to fit through the doorway of his shop.

What did he do? He knocked down part of the wall to get it out. He wasn't going to allow the door's limitations to limit *him*.

Trying to improve your life and tapping into your potential for success without pushing your limitations is like building a car in a small shed and choosing not to knock out a wall to get it out on the road. All locked up, your potential for success can't really go anywhere.

Remove the limitations and the world is open to you.

"We spend most of our twenties discovering all of the hundreds of things we can be. But as we mature into our thirties, we begin to discover all of the things we will never be. The challenge for us as we reach our forties and beyond is to put it all together—to know our capabilities and recognize our limitations— and become the best we can be."

—Catherine B. Ahles

HARNESS UNSTOPPABLE ENERGY

What most often stops you from doing what you want to do? Many people cite a lack of time: "I wish I had more hours in the day."

There's a problem with that thought. You can't change time! You can't get more, no matter what you do. The number of minutes in a day, days in a week, and weeks in a year is set. Even your time here on Earth is fixed. Everyone's days are numbered.

There are many limitations you can push in life. There are many talents you can develop, skills you can improve, and capacities you can increase.

Time is not one of them.

What should you do? Give up?

Never!

Focus on managing and harnessing your energy instead.

"The ultimate measure of our lives is not how much time we spend on the planet, but rather how much energy we invest in the time that we have...Performance, health, and happiness are grounded in the skillful management of energy...The number of hours in a day is fixed, but the quantity and quality of energy available to us is not. It is our most precious resource. The more we take responsibility for the energy we bring to the world, the more empowered and productive we become. The more we blame others or external circumstances, the more negative and compromised our energy is likely to be."

—Jim Loehr and Tony Schwartz

If you want to get more done
and make a greater impact on the world,
increase your energy capacity
and expend it wisely.

YOUR GREATEST
SOURCE OF ENERGY

People who reach their potential for success do not sit back and wait for things to happen to them. They go out and make things happen. That takes energy. Where do they get it?

One of the best sources of energy is knowing your purpose and focusing your effort in that area.
Doing what you believe you were made for will give you almost unlimited amounts of energy. Why? Because it rewards you internally. The same is true for doing what you do well. If something gives you a high return for your effort, not only do you get a lot done, but you feel good doing it.

Your goal in life should be to align your strengths and your efforts.

If...

What you HAVE to do,
What you are MADE to do,
What you are GLAD to do, and
What you are GREAT at doing

...all line up, you will always have energy.

"When you are fully charged, you get more done. You have better interactions. Your mind is sharp, and your body is strong. On days when you are fully charged, you experience high levels of engagement and well-being. This charge carries forward, creating an upward cycle for those you care about."

—Tom Rath

WHAT WEARS YOU DOWN?

What depletes your energy? Do you know? Have you paid attention to what sucks the life out of you?

Do you avoid those things as much as possible? You should.

Were you raised believing that you can accomplish *anything* as long as you try hard enough? It's not true. **Your potential is unlimited, but you have to acknowledge that you can never be your best in an area where you have no talent.**

"IN MATTERS OF STYLE,
SWIM WITH THE CURRENT;
IN MATTERS OF PRINCIPLE,
STAND LIKE A ROCK."

—old adage

Don't spend your life trying to be what you're not. Instead, try to be more of who you are naturally. Develop your natural strengths. It's the difference between going with the current and swimming against it. If you spend your time working in your weaknesses, you'll be swimming against the current every day of your life. That will always deplete your energy.

If you have a responsibility, fulfill it. Aside from that, avoid what wears you down. **Stay with your strengths and you'll go far.**

"Without intermittent recovery, we're not physiologically capable of sustaining highly positive emotions for long periods. Confronted with relentless demands and unexpected challenges, people tend to slip into negative emotions—the fight-or-flight mode— often multiple times in a day. They become irritable and impatient, or anxious and insecure. Such states of mind drain people's energy and cause friction in their relationships. Fight-or-flight emotions also make it impossible to think clearly, logically, and reflectively. When executives learn to recognize what kinds of events trigger their negative emotions, they gain greater capacity to take control of their reactions."

—Tony Schwartz and Catherine McCarthy

WHAT ARE YOUR REENERGIZERS?

No matter how much you stay with your strengths and avoid working in your weaknesses, you'll still get tired. What can you do about it? **Know what reenergizes you!**

What activities reinvigorate you? What ideas fire you up? Which people put fuel in your tank? Almost anything can boost your energy as long as it touches you in a positive way. Know what things give you energy.

The key is being intentional about connecting with them.

Be especially aware of what recharges your emotional, mental, and physical batteries: time alone or time with people. Even if you're a people person, you need to pay attention to who gives you energy and who drains it.

"YOUR WELL-BEING IS MORE DRAMATICALLY AFFECTED BY THE PEOPLE YOU SEE EVERY DAY, PEOPLE WHO LIVE WITHIN A FEW BLOCKS OF YOUR HOUSE, PEOPLE WHO LIVE WITHIN A FEW MILES, THAN IT IS BY DISTANT CONNECTIONS."

—Tom Rath

IDENTIFY WHEN YOU NEED TO RALLY YOUR ENERGY

Every day, there will be times when you don't have to be sharp; you can function almost on autopilot. But there will be other times when you need high energy to be at your best. **Knowing which is which and planning ahead are crucial to success.**

Most parts of your day don't require high energy:
When you're brushing your teeth. When you're eating breakfast.
When you're driving to or from work. When you're reading emails.
When you're taking out the trash.

But there are times when it's vital to increase your energy as much as possible: When you're meeting with a client. When you're making decisions that will impact your company. When you're coaching an employee. When you're having an important conversation with your spouse. When your child needs you. In such moments, you need to be "on," and that takes energy.

It's impossible for anyone to be full of energy
every minute of the entire day.

That's why you need to know when you
should marshal your energy.

Every day, look at your calendar and determine the times that will be what Jeffrey Gitomer calls "showtime": the interactions when what you say, do, and think are crucial to your personal, business, or relational success. You need to know when it's showtime every day in your life. It doesn't matter if these times occur once or a dozen times in your day, whether at 6 a.m. or midnight. You need to show up and give them 100 percent of your energy.

If you use your energy when you need it and conserve it when you don't, you can develop unstoppable energy.

CREATE MARGIN

No matter how well you plan, life happens. You need to make room for it.

Give yourself space in your schedule for the unexpected—both the positive and the negative. Having margin will keep you from overexpending your energy when difficulties arise, and it will help you pursue opportunities when you find them.

"It's extremely important not to have one's life all blocked out, not to have the days and weeks totally organized. It's essential to leave gaps and interludes for spontaneous action, for it is often in spontaneity and surprises that we open ourselves to unlimited opportunities and new areas brought into our lives by chance."

—Jean Hersey

Never assume your energy level is fixed.

You can manage it. You can increase it.

You can do more than you previously
believed you could do.

Dream big.

"THERE IS NO PASSION
TO BE FOUND PLAYING SMALL—
IN SETTLING FOR A LIFE
THAT IS LESS THAN
THE ONE YOU ARE
CAPABLE OF LIVING."

—Nelson Mandela

DEVELOP UNSTOPPABLE EMOTIONAL STRENGTH

Do you have emotional strength?

The answer lies in how well you handle adversity. Can you deal with failure, criticism, change, and pressure in a positive way? Do you easily bounce back from a setback?

If the answer is yes, you have an advantage. Keep working to make it better. If the answer is no, don't be discouraged, because you can improve your emotional strength. **It's a skill *anyone* can learn.**

THE KEY TO EMOTIONAL STRENGTH

If you were to boil emotional strength down to one word, what would it be?

Resilience.

"It's human nature to resist change—particularly when it comes in the form of adversity or challenges. But change is inevitable, and developing the trait of resilience helps us not only survive change, but also learn, grow, and thrive in it. Resilience is the capacity to cope with stress and adversity. It comes from believing in yourself and, at the same time, in something bigger than yourself. Resilience is not a trait that people are born with; it involves behaviors, thoughts, and actions that can be learned and developed in anyone."

—Lolly Daskal

"WITHOUT RESILIENCE,
THE FIRST FAILURE IS ALSO THE LAST—
BECAUSE IT'S FINAL."

—Eric Greitens

Resilient people are able to weather storms and recover from adversity. Why? They do not expect immediate results. Or instant success.

Remind yourself that you are in life for the long haul. You will experience struggles. Use your energy to encourage yourself to keep moving forward with fortitude.

START WITH
A CLEAN SLATE

One thing you can do to develop emotional strength is to start every day fresh. Give yourself a clean slate emotionally.

Don't hold on to old emotional baggage and carry it into the next day. **Let today be a new day.**

"ERASE THE BOARD
OF YOUR ACHIEVEMENTS
AND ALLOW YOURSELF
TO BE A BEGINNER AGAIN."

—James Fayal, inspired by Steve Jobs

"Many of life's annoyances just have to be ignored. That doesn't mean that we suppress, ignore, or deny every pain. Serious pain has to be confronted. But one mark of resilience is learning to tell which pain deserves our attention. Paying attention to every pain, all the time, doesn't lead to resilience. It usually just leads to whining."

—Eric Greitens

DON'T LET YOUR HIGHS OR LOWS CONTROL YOUR LIFE

Every day has the promise of a victory that can make you want to celebrate.

Every day also contains the potential for something negative that can threaten to wear you down emotionally.

To be successful, don't allow the highs of your positives or the lows of your negatives to take you too far out of a steady rhythm.

"HE WHO RULES HIS SPIRIT
IS BETTER THAN
HE WHO TAKES A CITY."

—Proverbs 16:32

You probably know you shouldn't let your lows take you down too far because they can make you discouraged. But did you know you shouldn't let your highs take you too high either? If you hold on to your successes for too long, you can become complacent. You can begin to feel entitled, lose perspective, and stop working hard. You might start putting more energy into protecting what you have instead of working hard to keep moving forward.

How can you limit the impact of highs and lows? Practice the twenty-four-hour rule.

When you achieve success, celebrate, but for no longer than twenty-four hours. After that, get back to work. Yesterday's success won't bring you tomorrow's success.

When you fail, allow yourself to be disappointed. Examine what went wrong. Learn from it. But after twenty-four hours, get back to work. Yesterday's failure doesn't define you. It doesn't have to stop you from achieving tomorrow's success.

"If I feel depressed I will sing.
If I feel sad I will laugh.
If I feel ill I will double my labor.
If I feel fear I will plunge ahead.
If I feel inferior I will wear new garments.
If I feel uncertain I will raise my voice.
If I feel poverty I will think of wealth to come.
If I feel incompetent I will remember
past success.
If I feel insignificant I will remember my goals.
Today I will be master of my emotions."

—Og Mandino

DON'T WASTE ENERGY ON THINGS YOU CAN'T CONTROL

Controlling what you can and not wasting energy on what you can't is one of the most important lessons you can learn in life.

Don't waste your energy emotionally when you're stuck in bad traffic, lose your luggage, or get caught in a storm. These and many other factors are beyond your control. Instead, focus on what you *can* control.

What can you control?

Your Attitude

Your Choices

Your Priorities

Your Passion

Your Growth

Your Actions

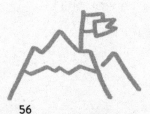

"YOU MUST UNDERSTAND
THE DIFFERENCE BETWEEN
A FACT OF LIFE AND A PROBLEM.
A FACT OF LIFE IS SOMETHING YOU
CANNOT CONTROL OR FIX. A PROBLEM
IS SOMETHING YOU CAN FIX."

—Fred Smith

LEARN FROM YOUR MISTAKES

It's been said that the definition of insanity is doing the same thing over and over but expecting different results.

If you hope for different results but never change your actions, you will wear yourself out emotionally.

What's a better path?

When you don't get the results you want, ask yourself why.
Successful people make plenty of mistakes, but they take the time
to learn from them.

"NO MAN CAN PRODUCE GREAT THINGS WHO IS NOT THOROUGHLY SINCERE IN DEALING WITH HIMSELF."

—James Russell Lowell

The next time you fall short, don't run from it.

Examine it.

Review it.

Reflect on it.

Learn from it.

Redirect your actions based on what you learn, and take action—different action. Instead of feeling exhausted by your failure, you'll feel encouraged by your progress, however small it may be.

DON'T ALLOW OTHERS TO CONTROL YOUR RELATIONSHIPS

Be aware of how your relationships impact you emotionally. People with emotional strength honor their relationships. They fulfill their responsibilities as child, parent, spouse, friend, neighbor. At the same time, they guard against letting others control them.

Love others. Be yourself. Do what is right. Don't let anyone else try to make you into someone you're not.

"THE EASIEST THING TO BE
IN THE WORLD IS YOU.
THE MOST DIFFICULT THING
TO BE IS WHAT OTHER PEOPLE
WANT YOU TO BE. DON'T LET THEM
PUT YOU IN THAT POSITION."

—Leo Buscaglia

BOUNCE BACK!

Every week of your life, you will be hit in the gut by unwanted surprises. You will be blindsided by negative relationships. You will be knocked down by a blow you didn't see coming.

The best you can do when you get knocked down is to get back up and keep going. By taking action, you can pull yourself out of the pit you find yourself in.

Hoping, wishing, denying, crying, cussing, fussing, moaning, blaming, and waiting only keep you in the pit.

The faster you can recover from the shock of the emotion, process through it, and move toward action, the quicker your recovery time will be. And the more emotionally strong you will become.

The choice is always yours. You must continually work on mastering your emotions or you will be mastered by them.

BECOME AN UNSTOPPABLE THINKER

"NOTHING LIMITS ACHIEVEMENT
LIKE SMALL THINKING;
NOTHING EXPANDS POSSIBILITIES
LIKE UNLEASHED IMAGINATION."

—William Arthur Ward

Two people can see the same things, go through the same experiences, have the same conversations, yet one walks away with a flurry of great thoughts and the other without a single new idea. What's the difference between them?

The first has the mindset of someone who never stops thinking. The other doesn't.

To become an unstoppable thinker, you need to be an observer. You need to become a miner of ideas. And you have to be willing to think big.

Success is difficult, if not impossible,
without the ability to think better.

What will make your thinking unstoppable?

"YOU ARE TODAY WHERE
YOUR THOUGHTS HAVE
BROUGHT YOU; YOU WILL BE
TOMORROW WHERE
YOUR THOUGHTS TAKE YOU."

—James Allen

EVALUATE YOUR THINKING

How do you know a good idea is really a *good* idea?

It lasts more than twenty-four hours.

Bad ideas are like fish left out on a counter. After twenty-four hours, they stink!

If you're not certain how to evaluate an idea, allow it to rest a day or two, then ask yourself these questions:

- Does my idea still speak to me?

- Will this thought speak to others?

- How, where, and when can I use this thought?

- Who can this thought help?

If you don't have positive answers to these questions, the idea's probably not worth pursuing—at least, not in its current form.

CAPTURE YOUR THOUGHTS

The majority of people who have great ideas never implement them. Why? Because they never put them in writing.

Capturing your thinking in words does three things for you.

First, it helps you to remember. How many times have you said, "I had a great idea this morning (or last night, or in the shower, or during a meeting), but I can't remember what it was." When you take the time to write down your ideas, you'll never say that again.

Second, writing your idea helps you to think it through more clearly.

Third, if you write it down and keep track of it, you'll never again waste time trying to recall it or track it down. Decide what subject it falls under and file it.

"LEARNING TO WRITE IS LEARNING TO THINK. YOU DON'T KNOW ANYTHING CLEARLY UNLESS YOU CAN STATE IT IN WRITING."

—S. I. Hayakawa

RAISE THE BAR

There isn't a single idea that starts out as good as it can be. Every idea you imagine can be taken to another level.

Once you've determined that an idea is worth pursuing, revisit it. How can you improve it? How can you connect it? How can you maximize it? How can you share it?

Developed ideas are always stronger than bright ideas.

"A good idea is a bad idea
turned upside down."

—Linda Kaplan Thaler

SHARE YOUR THINKING

To get the most out of an idea, you need to do more than just think it through. You need to share it with other good thinkers and talk it out.

Don't try to hold on to an idea until it's "finished." Share it with others and invite them to finish it with you:

- Talking expresses your heart.

- Talking tests your idea.

- Talking expands your idea.

- Talking invites input from others.

You learn a lot when you present an idea to others, especially when they're people who don't know you well or who won't automatically give you the benefit of the doubt. Share your thinking with strangers and skeptics and you'll find out where you really stand.

The ultimate shared-thinking experience occurs when you bring a good idea to the table with a small group of good thinkers. They will always make your thoughts better.

OWN YOUR IDEAS

Something powerful happens when you move from *believing* in an idea to *owning* it.

When you *believe* in an idea, it's like investing in an endeavor with someone else's money. You give it a try and you hope it works.

When you *own* an idea, it's like putting your own money into the investment. You become willing to do what it takes to make it work. The greater the investment, the more dedicated you become to seeing it through.

"AN IDEA CAN TURN
TO DUST OR MAGIC,
DEPENDING ON THE TALENT
THAT RUBS AGAINST IT."

—William Bernbach

Thinking better will increase
your potential, maximize your capacity,
and make you more successful.

It gives a greater return than working harder.

CULTIVATE UNSTOPPABLE CREATIVITY

If you consider yourself a creative person, you probably work in your creative lane every day of your life.
But what if you don't think of yourself that way? Then it's even more important for you to cultivate creativity, because it can greatly improve your life.

People with creative confidence make better choices. They set off more easily in new directions. They are better able to find solutions to seemingly intractable problems. They continually see new possibilities and effectively collaborate with others to improve the situations around them. A person who cultivates an unstoppable creativity discovers newfound courage to approach big challenges.

Wouldn't you like to have all those positive possibilities?

"CREATIVITY IS NOT A TALENT.
IT IS A WAY OF OPERATING."

—John Cleese

Don't fret if you don't think of yourself as a *creative*.
You don't have to be an artist or an inventor to be creative.
You just need to open yourself up to greater creativity or tap
into the creativity you had when you were younger.

You can rekindle the creativity that's already in you. You can
cultivate new pathways of creativity. You can unleash new
possibilities in you. **There are things you can do to tap
into your creativity.**

"All children are artists,
and it is an indictment of
our culture that so many of them
lose their creativity,
their unfettered imaginations,
as they grow older."

—Madeleine L'Engle

"STUFF YOUR HEAD
WITH MORE DIFFERENT THINGS
FROM VARIOUS FIELDS."

—Ray Bradbury

CONNECT THE UNCONNECTED

Your biggest creative breakthrough will occur when you discover that creativity is really about connecting things that don't seem to go together naturally.

A fantastic way to do that is to collect ideas and quotes.
When you set your mind to identify and record great ideas as you
read a book, listen to a podcast, or watch a film, you heighten your
awareness. When you prompt yourself to categorize that idea, you
make connections. When you think about how or where you can
use an idea, you make additional connections. Do that all the time
and you will train your mind to think in new ways. You begin to
think more strategically and creatively.

The next time you're trying to be innovative or to take an idea to
another level, focus on the challenge, problem, or process, and
look for ways to make connections to it. How can you take that
idea and connect it with experiences, people, other ideas, quotes,
stories, opportunities, or questions? **Don't limit your thinking
in any way.**

> "CREATIVITY IS JUST CONNECTING THINGS."
>
> —Steve Jobs

CREATIVE ≠ UNDISCIPLINED

People who resist creativity often have a misconception about it. They see being creative as haphazard, random, or undisciplined. It doesn't have to be that way.

You don't have to wait for a muse to be creative. In fact, people who practice creativity don't wait for it. They schedule it.

"I WRITE ONLY WHEN INSPIRATION STRIKES. FORTUNATELY, IT STRIKES EVERY MORNING AT 9:00 A.M. SHARP."

—Attributed to William Faulkner

Find a place where you *believe* you can be creative, and then schedule time to be there and reach for it. Even if you don't feel any inspiration, by showing up, you may *become* inspired.

The discipline of being available to create will give you the opportunity to create. And eventually, you will develop the *habit* of creating.

ASK QUESTIONS TO SPARK IDEAS

One of the best things you can do to cultivate unstoppable creativity is to ask questions. Why? Because questions cause you to explore. They make you seek out new ideas and information.

Make *why* one of your favorite words.

Make *what if* one of your favorite phrases.

Make *How can we take this to another level?* one of your favorite questions.

Even mundane questions can sometimes lead to breathtakingly creative answers.

BELIEVE THERE IS ALWAYS AN ANSWER

Creativity is a mindset. You have to believe that answers and solutions exist—if you are willing to search for them and keep fighting to find them.

The words *reactive* and *creative* are made up of exactly the same letters. The only difference between the two is where we place the *c*. Decide that you will *c* (see) things differently!

Are you willing to believe that every challenge *always* has an answer? No matter what the situation is? No matter how difficult it seems? No matter how high the stakes?

When you believe there is an answer, you're not being stubborn; you're practicing possibilities.

Creativity is changing the question you ask from "Is there an answer?" to "What is the answer?"

"I'm a genetic optimist.
I've been told, 'Jeff, you're fooling
yourself; the problem is unsolvable.'
But I don't think so.
It just takes a lot of time,
patience, and experimentation."

—Jeff Bezos

BELIEVE THERE IS MORE THAN ONE ANSWER

Once you've mastered the shift from "Is there an answer?" to "What is the answer?" you'll be ready to make *another* creative leap. Start believing there is always *more than one* answer.

That's the creative shift from no option to one option to many options.

When you shift into creative mode, begin thinking broadly and searching for as many answers as possible. Only when you develop a long list of options should you line them up and ask, "What is the *best* option?" The greater the *number* of possibilities, the greater the *possibilities*!

By being flexible and demonstrating the ability to adapt to fluctuating situations with many options, you will be more effective and productive. **Your creativity will multiply dramatically when you always believe there are many answers to any problem.**

BELIEVE THAT EVERYTHING AND EVERYONE CAN GET BETTER

Creative people, whether they are artists, inventors, businesspeople, or teachers, believe there are always better ways to do things.

When you believe that everyone and everything can get better, it gives you confidence that you can help people and make a difference. And it inspires you to keep looking for ways to solve problems and pursue opportunities.

"WE STAY IN BUSINESS BECAUSE
WE CONTINUE TO CREATE.
NOTHING THAT WORKED YESTERDAY
WILL WORK TODAY."

—Bob Hammer

LET GO OF OLD IDEAS AND EMBRACE NEW ONES

If you are already successful, one of the most important things you'll ever do is to be willing to say yesterday's thinking is tired, outdated, or flat-out wrong.

Creativity, in its nature, is embracing something new.

"IT'S EASY TO COME UP
WITH NEW IDEAS; THE HARD PART
IS LETTING GO OF WHAT WORKED
FOR YOU TWO YEARS AGO
BUT WILL SOON BE OUT OF DATE."

—Roger von Oech

When most people have worked hard on something, they usually have a hard time letting it go. Creativity demands that we release our grip on something old to grasp something new. Writer Sir Arthur Quiller-Couch called this process "killing your darlings."

When was the last time you said goodbye to something that used to be special but that no longer works today?

"Don't cap your expectations!
What you define as impossible today is
impossible only in the context of present
paradigms. But maybe we should let
William Wordsworth have the last word
on this subject of the untapped promise
that lies within us all. Speaking of his fellow
humans, he said simply, 'We are greater
than we know.' It's true for us as individuals,
as institutions, and as a society.
We can only guess at our true potential.
And we can only achieve it if we get past
the paradigms and unleash our imaginations."

—Monte Haymon

COLLABORATE

One of the greatest barriers to creativity comes from holding back ideas from others instead of sharing them. Why? Because collaboration is perhaps the greatest creative stimulant of all.

Do you protect your ideas and keep them to yourself? Is it because you want to perfect them first? Or make them "presentable"? Are you worried that your ideas will be rejected? Do you worry that you won't get the credit? Or that your ideas will be stolen?

Collaboration is a big risk. But its rewards are bigger.

The sooner you get other perspectives on your thinking, the closer you will come to finding better ideas and answers.

"NONE OF US IS AS SMART AS ALL OF US."

—Ken Blanchard

As you work to take ideas to another level, use this three-*E* formula for collaborative creativity:

> *Exposure* of an idea to the right people
> + *Expression* from their different perspectives
> = *Expansion* of that idea beyond your personal ability.

Do that and you will not only increase your creativity, but you will also inspire the people who work for you to unleash theirs too.

"THE BIGGEST SINGLE VARIABLE OF WHETHER OR NOT EMPLOYEES WILL BE CREATIVE IS WHETHER THEY PERCEIVE THEY HAVE PERMISSION."

—David Hills

If you desire to cultivate your creativity and tap into greater potential for success, you can do it.

You can train yourself to see possibilities. You can learn to find answers. You can become someone who always offers options. You can work with others to become inventive and innovative.

FOSTER

UNSTOPPABLE

RELATIONSHIPS

People can usually trace their successes and failures to the relationships in their lives.

The most important decision you can make in your *personal life* is to foster good relationships with your family, friends, and neighbors.

The most important decision you can make in your *professional life* is to develop great long-term relationships with people who can help you make a difference.

How can you foster beautiful, productive, long-term relationships that greatly improve your life? Change your focus from *me* to *we*.

Relational capacity is key to personal and professional success. **When you're good with people, you're unstoppable.**

"IT MARKS A BIG STEP IN YOUR
DEVELOPMENT WHEN YOU
COME TO REALIZE THAT
OTHER PEOPLE CAN HELP YOU
DO A BETTER JOB
THAN YOU COULD DO ALONE."

—Andrew Carnegie

Fostering unstoppable relationships with people really does make a huge difference. Your interactions with others will go to a new level when you realize how much you need the right people in your life.

You receive the help of people when you're willing to say, "I need you." You can't be successful alone. You must have the help of others.

Ask for help. And don't assume others will say no. People want to help someone who can't make it without them.

VALUE EVERY PERSON EVERY DAY

You can't foster great relationships unless you value people and care about them. If you don't like people, don't respect them, and don't believe they have value, you will always experience a barrier between you and them.

You can't secretly look down on others and build them up at the same time.

How you value people always shows through.

"EVERY DAY, INTENTIONALLY VALUE PEOPLE, BELIEVE IN PEOPLE, AND UNCONDITIONALLY LOVE THEM."

—Melvin Maxwell

All people desire to have someone who loves them, believes in them, and is there for them.

If you're willing to be that kind of friend to others, not only will you become great at building relationships, but you will also gain a more satisfying life.

CHOOSE TO BELIEVE THE BEST ABOUT EVERYONE

Believing the best in others is always the right thing to do, even if it means you may not always be right.

Try to see people as they could be, not necessarily as they are. When you believe the best in people, you won't feel compelled to correct them or try to fix them. Instead, you will be able to validate and encourage them.

"I ALWAYS PREFER TO BELIEVE THE BEST OF EVERYBODY; IT SAVES SO MUCH TROUBLE."

—Attributed to Rudyard Kipling

When you're tempted to fix others, it's important to remember that you're not perfect either.

If you want to fix someone, fix yourself! Besides, people will be more apt to change when you believe in them rather than when you try to fix or change them.

SEE EVERYONE AS A TEN!

You have a choice when it comes to how you see other people.

When you meet people, are your expectations high for some and low for others? What if you started out seeing everyone as a ten? How would your interactions with people change for the better?

Will everyone remain a ten? Maybe not. You can begin a relationship with a *belief* number of ten, but your *experience* with a person may lower that. If someone treats others well, keeps their word, adds value to people, demonstrates high competence, and so on, the number will remain high. On the other hand, if the person is self-centered, dysfunctional, abusive, or negative, then the number will go down. But why not start everyone out as a ten?

GIVE MORE
THAN YOU TAKE

To build great relationships, you need to want more *for* people than you want *from* people.

When you want more for others and give more than you take, you become a plus in other people's lives. When you take more, you become a minus. That's simple relational math.

Never assume you're being a plus in a relationship unless you are intentionally giving.

It's never good to take *any* relationship for granted. Relationships never stay the same. And they won't thrive if left alone. They need cultivation. If you intentionally and regularly add value, you will continue being a plus in another person's life. And when you're giving, not just taking, the relationship has the potential to keep moving forward and improving.

MAKE THE FIRST MOVE

Don't expect people to come to you. Make the first move and go to them first.

Be intentional and show initiative by moving toward the relationships you desire. If you wait for the right people to approach you, you may never meet them.

Once someone is part of your life, keep making yourself available. Let them know what they mean to you. Sometimes you don't even need to say a word. Just being there is enough.

"Too often we underestimate the power of a touch, a smile, a kind word, a listening ear, an honest compliment, or the smallest act of caring, all of which have the potential to turn a life around."

—Leo Buscaglia

"DEEP DOWN IN
EVERY HUMAN HEART
THERE IS MERCY
AND GENEROSITY."

—Nelson Mandela

WIN TOUGH RELATIONSHIPS

Let's face it. Not everyone is easy to love. Some people are even difficult to *like*. Debbie Ellis described extending yourself to and valuing such people as being like trying to hug a porcupine!

Your ultimate goal should be to treat others better than they treat you, to add value to them in a greater capacity than they may expect or deserve.

Is it easy? No. Is it possible? Yes!

Nelson Mandela is a great example of someone who did this. Brian Bethune said of Mandela: "He was greater than his enemies deserved; greater than the leaders of foot-dragging Western countries who later rushed to eulogize him; greater than his family, squabbling about his legacy."

"LOVE ONE ANOTHER
AND YOU WILL BE HAPPY.
IT'S AS SIMPLE AND AS
DIFFICULT AS THAT."

—Michael Leunig

**Helping people is always
worth the effort.**

What if you're not naturally a people person?

Then this may be more challenging for you than it is for someone who is naturally good with people. But you can still become better at building relationships and increase your people capacity.

The more you value people, put yourself into their world, work to add value to them, and be a friend, the better your life will be. The more you will increase your potential. And the more successful you have the potential to be.

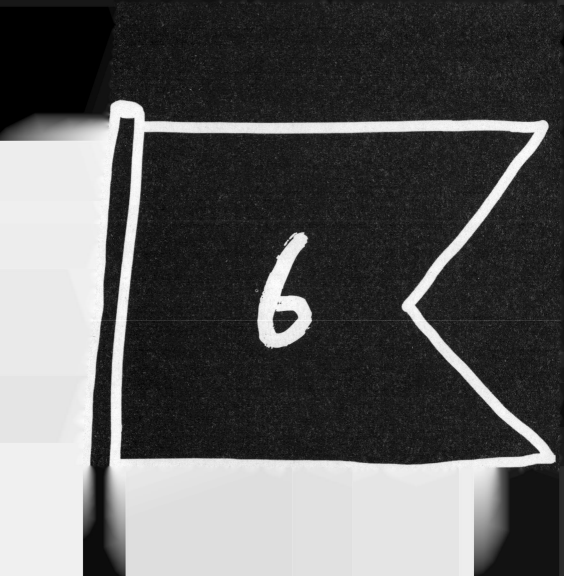

ACCOMPLISH UNSTOPPABLE RESULTS

You will reach your potential and be
successful only if you achieve results.
You already know this.

But do you believe you have the ability
to accomplish great results?
Unstoppable results?

You should. Because among all the ways you can tap into your potential to become the unstoppable you, the one *least* dependent on natural ability is results:

- You don't need to be a genius to achieve results.

- You don't need to be talented to achieve results.

- You don't need to be rich to achieve results.

- You don't need to be experienced to achieve results.

- You don't need to be educated to achieve results.

- You don't need to be lucky to achieve results.

You need only to be willing to work for it!

The world will try to talk you out of working hard. Negative people will try to convince you that you can't get ahead. They might even tell you that others have already beaten you down, the system is rigged, and they are on top because they have stepped on you.

Don't believe it. You may *feel* down, but you don't have to *be* down. Or *stay* down.

BE READY TO CLIMB

Everything worthwhile in life—everything you want, everything you desire to achieve, everything you want to receive—is uphill.

The problem for most people is that they have uphill dreams but downhill habits.

You cannot slide your way to success. Nobody can.

THE DIFFERENCE
BETWEEN A LIFE OF
UPHILL CLIMBING AND
DOWNHILL SLIDING

UPHILL CLIMBING

Everything Worthwhile
High Self-Respect
Positive Momentum
Wins
High Morale
Making a Difference
Self-Improvement
Purposeful
Fulfilling

DOWNHILL SLIDING

Nothing Worthwhile
Low Self-Esteem
Negative Momentum
Losses
Low Morale
Not Making a Difference
No Improvement
Aimless
Empty

Are you willing to work for an uphill life?
That's the question.

Everything worthwhile is uphill.
Let that really sink in.
Here are the implications of that statement:

EVERYTHING

That's inclusive. It means it's all-encompassing.
Nothing in your life is exempt.

WORTHWHILE

This means anything desirable, advisable, appropriate, good for you.

UPHILL

This means your experience is going to be rugged, punishing, strenuous, exhausting.

Downhill is easy. It has no requirements. It doesn't take any effort. It's like giving in to the effects of gravity, which continually pull us down. You can *slide* downhill—in your sleep. A downhill lifestyle is characterized by unintentionality, complacency, inconsistency, and excuses. It has no big-picture vision for the future, only instant gratification. It requires no thought, choice, or action. It just lets go and waits.

Moving uphill requires intentionality, energy, determination, hard work, and consistency.
It's hard. It requires you to keep an eye on the big picture. You must remain determined and put in the time.

The right thing to do and the hard thing to do are usually the same thing.

More and more people resist doing the right thing because it's hard. Instead, they do the easy thing. They go downhill instead of uphill as a result. Don't join them!

"The tragedy of life is often not in our failure, but rather in our complacency; not in our doing too much, but rather in our doing too little; not in our living above our ability, but rather in our living below our capacities."

—Benjamin E. Mays

Your challenge is to change from what you have done to what you are capable of doing.

Perhaps you find that intimidating. Maybe you've not done as well in the past as you'd have liked to. And you find it difficult to move forward when it comes to accomplishing results. If you think you can't do it for yourself, will you attempt it for your family, your friends, and your teammates? The life you choose *for* you doesn't begin and end *with* you. What you do impacts many people.

If you feel like your life is going downhill instead of up toward the results and rewards you desire, change the way you work. **Embrace uphill practices and habits that will help you to increase your capacity.**

VISUALIZE YOUR IDEAL RESULTS

Do you have a vision for what you want to accomplish? Have you created a mental model of what you desire to achieve? If not, you need to work on that. Your picture of ideal results is your starting point.

As you imagine the results you want to achieve, put as much detail into the picture as you can. Will you achieve the perfect goal you desire? Probably not. **But the picture of your ideal destination is where you need to start.**

"BEGIN WITH
THE END IN MIND."

—Stephen R. Covey

START WORKING BEFORE YOU HAVE ALL THE ANSWERS

After you've thought about the perfect ending to your efforts, you face a real danger: thinking you have to know the perfect way to get there. Don't fall into that trap! **If you wait until you have all the answers to start working, you'll never start.**

Yes, you need to have a vision for what you're trying to do, but you also have to be willing to take action in the face of uncertainty. Unstoppable people possess a bias for action. That's how they are so consistent in getting results.

Be willing to take a step forward.

And make it a small step. It's human nature to want to start an effort with a single bold, certain leap. Who wouldn't want a big head start, a quantum leap ahead? But there are very few quantum leaps in life.

If you're willing to take one small step, ten small steps, one hundred small steps, then you may someday get a chance to make a leap. Others may think you've become an overnight success, but you'll know it's the result of many small successes.

"A JOURNEY OF
A THOUSAND MILES
BEGINS WITH
A SINGLE STEP."

—Lao Tzu

Take that first uncertain step. Whatever you have—or don't have—figured out, be willing to start. You may not know all the steps between you and your final results, but you will be at least one step closer to what you want.

BE WILLING TO FAIL

To achieve results, you have to be willing to *not* achieve results every time you try. **In other words, you must be willing to fail.**

The willingness to make mistakes, fall down, look foolish, and fall short may seem to go against the goal of achieving ideal results. It's not. Everybody fails. The newer something is to you, the more likely you are to fail. So what? Go ahead and fail. Then try again.

To be productive, you have to be willing to fail. A lot.

Failure is not final. Just learn from it. Let what didn't work teach you what does.

STAY FOCUSED

How hard do you work at what you're trying to accomplish? How long do you stick with something to make it work? Do you hang in there for a long time, or do you give up easily?

If you have a habit of quitting, it's time to break it.

Don't dabble. Don't try to do two, three, or four things at once. Do the one thing you must achieve today to get you closer to the end result, and stick with it until it's done. You don't need talent, intelligence, resources, or opportunity to stick with it. **The only things you need are intentionality and perseverance.**

KEEP MOVING FORWARD

When you're focused on trying to accomplish results, how do you decide what you should do?

To get more done, don't think in terms of tasks being right or wrong, good or bad. Just ask yourself one question:

Will this action move me forward in the journey toward my vision?

Indecision freezes people and keeps them from being successful. Don't get bogged down in whether an action is the *best* one you can take. Evaluate quickly and take any positive action. If it moves you forward, it is a good choice.

When it comes to character and ethical decisions, yes, there is a right and a wrong. But when it comes to accomplishing results, there isn't. Something works, or it doesn't. It takes you forward, or it doesn't. It helps the team, or it doesn't.

EVALUATE YOUR RESULTS AND KEEP IMPROVING

If you want to keep accomplishing results, you need to keep improving. You will be able to do that only if you continually evaluate your work and make adjustments.

Don't wait until something is broken to evaluate it. Certainly do fix what's broken. But don't stop there. What's working that can be improved? What's successful that can teach you how to improve something else? What worked yesterday but should be scrapped to make way for tomorrow?

If you're not better today
than you were yesterday,
you're missing an opportunity.

And you won't be better tomorrow
if you don't find ways to improve today.

STOP DOING
WHAT YOU'RE NOT
GREAT AT DOING

When you're just starting out in your career, you have to do everything. You have very few choices about what you will and won't do. But the reality is that you will drastically increase your productivity and the results you accomplish if you stop doing what you're not great at and instead focus on what you do best.

Your goal as you advance in your career should be to eliminate anything that doesn't give you or your team a high return. This is the only time quitting makes sense.

Stop trying to do what you can't do. Start doing only what you do best. That's where you will see the greatest results. That will keep taking you uphill, to the place you long to go.

BUILD UNSTOPPABLE LEADERSHIP

At some point, as you strive to reach your potential and be more successful, you will come to a place where you are bumping up against your own personal limits. When you reach that moment, what will you do?

Don't give up. Your limits don't have to limit you.

Don't believe you've reached the end of your ability to grow and achieve.

Don't stop dreaming.

Instead, expand your capacity by building your **leadership**.

When you enlist and engage other like-minded people in what you're doing, you will multiply your own efforts. You become truly unstoppable.

FIND YOUR PEOPLE

How do you find the people you can lead to accomplish all you desire to do?

Stop talking and spend more time listening.

Communication is the language of leadership, and communication is a two-way street.

"THE GREAT ENEMY OF COMMUNICATION, WE FIND, IS THE ILLUSION OF IT."

—William H. Whyte

Ask questions. You don't find your people by giving directions. You don't discover like-minded people by giving answers. Don't try to impress others. Instead, ask questions. Questions are the keys that unlock the doors to other people's lives.

When you ask people questions, you place value on them. You begin to really *see* them. Your focus is on them.

And listen. Really listen. If questions unlock the door, listening keeps the door open. Questions start the conversation, but listening encourages it to continue. Listening shows that you want to understand someone before being understood by them.

Leadership is not about you.

Questions + Listening = Quality Conversation

Quality Conversation = Quality Leadership

"YOU'RE ONLY AS GOOD
AS THE PEOPLE YOU HIRE."

—Ray Kroc

LET PEOPLE KNOW YOU VALUE THEM

The only way to become an unstoppable leader is to continually value the people on your team and add value to them.

Let the people you work with know you care about them. Tell them. Show them you believe in them. It's wonderful when people believe in their leader, but it's more wonderful when their leader believes in them.

When you value people, you will naturally care for them. And you will invest in them. You will serve them.

You won't manipulate people for your advantage when you truly value them. Instead, you'll motivate them to help them reach their potential. The amazing thing is that when you help them reach their potential, their efforts will help you reach yours.

"If a leader demonstrates competency, genuine concern for others, and admirable character, people will follow."

—T. Richard Chase

HELP PEOPLE SEE THEIR OWN POTENTIAL

Nothing helps people win more than their belief in themselves. Self-worth is foundational to belief and growth. When people's belief in themselves goes up, so can their commitment to help themselves. People who see their own value invest in themselves.

If the people on your team don't believe in themselves, as their leader, you need to try to help them find that belief.

"GOOD LEADERS MUST FIRST BECOME GOOD SERVANTS."

—Robert K. Greenleaf

Look for their potential. Speak positive words of affirmation to them about what you see in them.

Teach them. Encourage them. Set them up for success by helping them put wins under their belts. As their self-worth rises, so will their performance and job satisfaction.

BE AUTHENTIC

One of the most valuable things you can do to increase your leadership capacity is to be authentic and transparent with the people you lead.

Share your story. Be yourself.

"WE ADOPTED A PHILOSOPHY THAT WE WOULDN'T HIDE ANYTHING, NOT ANY OF OUR PROBLEMS, FROM THE EMPLOYEES."

—Rollin King

Too many leaders think they need to project a perfect image to have leadership credibility. They think they always have to put their best foot forward. What they don't understand is that even their best foot is a flawed foot. They don't understand the power of their own stories of imperfection. Your story of struggle, growth, and improvement actually increases your credibility. It has the power to inspire people and change lives.

Being authentic takes courage. But the results are worth the risk.

People respect leaders who tell the truth and at the same time still hold fast to the vision and keep leading the team forward.

"It is one of the most beautiful compensations of life that no [one] can sincerely try to help another without helping himself."

—Ralph Waldo Emerson

INITIATE CONNECTION WITH PEOPLE

By its nature, leadership is about creating change.
When you lead others, you invite them to change their focus, change their energy, change their skills, and sometimes even change their direction in life. You ask them to adapt for the sake of the team and the accomplishment of the vision. How can you get people to trust you enough to make so many changes?

Trust starts with good relationships. Good relationships start with good connection.

To initiate connection, go to others rather than expecting them to come to you. Then find what you have in common. Search for it. Keep your eyes open. Ask questions. Your common ground could be topical, experiential, geographical, emotional, physical, historical, philosophical, or theological. It doesn't have to be significant. It may even seem trivial at first.

Don't force it or rush it. But explore it, find it, and connect through it.

ASK PEOPLE TO JOIN YOU AFTER YOU'VE BUILT THE RELATIONSHIP

Your focus will often be on the vision, the agenda, the project, or the next task. All of those things are important. And you will need to communicate them. But you risk the vision if you haven't connected with people before asking them to help you.

People will be more likely to hear what you say and see what you see if they have connected with who you are. For that reason, a good leader always touches the heart before asking for a hand.

If you are transparent with how you feel about the vision, your people will respect you. If you have connected with them before asking them for help, they will follow you.

ASK, "WILL YOU HELP ME?"

Followership is voluntary. Even people who work *for* you don't have to work *with* you.

"YOU DO NOT LEAD
BY HITTING PEOPLE
OVER THE HEAD—
THAT'S ASSAULT,
NOT LEADERSHIP."

—Dwight D. Eisenhower

Most people respond well if you ask them for help.
Everyone would rather be invited than ordered to do something,
and few say no. If people refuse, you know where they stand. If they
say yes, you have their buy-in, and you can measure their level of
participation and commitment. If they don't follow through, you
can hold them accountable.

**Once they've said yes, be ready to answer two questions:
What do you want them to *know*, and what do you want
them to *do*?**

"It is important to focus on a shared vision of success up front. This is a preventative measure. When expectations are not clearly defined up front, trust and speed both go down. A lot of time is wasted due to leaders not clearly defining expectations. Failure to clarify expectations leaves people guessing. When results are delivered they fall short and are not valued."

—Stephen R. Covey

"LEADERSHIP ISN'T
WIELDING AUTHORITY.
IT'S EMPOWERING PEOPLE."

—Becky Bodin

HELP YOUR PEOPLE SUCCEED

As a leader, your task is to help the members of your team succeed. Set them up for success. Remove obstacles. Train them. Develop them. Coach them. Every time they win, celebrate.

"IT IS ONLY AS WE DEVELOP OTHERS THAT WE PERMANENTLY SUCCEED."

—Harvey S. Firestone

The people you lead will get better only by making changes. No one has ever risen to a higher level while staying the same. Being willing to change is one of the prices your people must pay to grow.

Help your team recognize and accept that price. Help them by investing in them and empowering them to improve. And when they experience bumps in the road or discouragement, come alongside them, assist them, and encourage them.

A win for a team member is a win for the team and for you.

Judge your success as a leader by how much you are able to help others. In the end, life is about people. Never forget it.

Take care of your people instead of taking care of your career.

If you are willing to do the work to build your leadership capacity, and you're willing to do it for the sake of others by adding value to them, you will find your life to be greatly rewarding.

KEEP
CLIMBING
HIGHER

On the journey to reaching your potential, you are truly unstoppable. Why? Because your potential can never be entirely fulfilled. Anywhere in your life you have potential, you have the possibility of *greater* potential. There is no finish line. Don't put limits on yourself that God and nature haven't. **I hope you now realize that your life need not have limits.**

"NOTHING IS MORE COMMON THAN UNFULFILLED POTENTIAL."

—Howard Hendricks

These seven ways to tap into your potential are only the beginning. Keep searching for others that are significant to who you are as a unique individual.

As long as you're breathing, you have places to go and ways to grow. You can always continue to improve. You can do more. You can make a greater difference. It's all within your reach. My hope and prayer is that you'll keep reaching until you accomplish something worthwhile...and then keep reaching for more.

Success isn't a place you reach. It's not a destination at which you can arrive. **Success is who you are if you keep striving toward your potential and keep growing.**

Keep climbing higher.

ACKNOWLEDGMENTS

I want to say thank you to Charlie Wetzel and the rest of the team who assisted me with the formation and publication of this book. And to the people in my organizations who support it. You all add incredible value to me, which allows me to add value to others. Together, we're making a difference!